SPIDERS

BY DAN GREENBERG

Benchmark Books

MARSHALL CAVENDISH
NEW YORK

Series Consultant:
James Doherty
General Curator
The Bronx Zoo, New York

With thanks to
Paul Zabarauskas.
Department of Entymology,
Wildlife Conservation Society, New York,
for his expert reading of this manuscript

Benchmark Books
Marshall Cavendish Corporation
99 White Plains Road
Tarrytown, NY 10591–9001
Website: www.marshallcavendish.com

Library of Congress Cataloging-in-Publication Data
Greenberg, Daniel A.
Spiders / by Dan Greenberg.
p. cm. – (Animals, animals)
Includes bibliographical references and index.
ISBN 0-7614-1263-8
1. Spiders–Juvenile literature. [1. Spiders.] I. Title. II. Series.

QL458.4.G76 2001   595.4′4–dc21   00-050739

Cover photo courtesy of *Animals Animals*: © Maria Zorn

All photographs are used by permission and through the courtesy of: *Animals Animals*: Bill Beatty, 43; G. Murray Bertram, Jr., 29; E.R. Degginger, 5; H. L. Fox, 27; Richard Kolar, 22; Ted Levin, 40; C. Milkins, 10 (left); O.S.F., 20 (bottom right), 24; Patti Murray, 20 (bottom left); James H. Robinson: 18; G. W. Willis: 13 (middle right); *Bruce Coleman Inc*: Alan Blank, 25; Jane Burton, 34; Dodge & Thompson, 38; Hans Reinhard, 20 (top center); *Peter Arnold, Inc*: Fred Bruemmer, 11; M & C Photography, 28; C. Allan Morgan, 13 (top left); Hans Pfletschinger, 20 (bottom center), 31, 35, 36; Horst Schaefer, 8; © *Robert & Linda Mitchell*: 9, 10 (right), 13 (bottom right), 20 (top left, top right), 21 (top left), 33, 37; *Visuals Unlimited, Inc*.: David G. Campbell, 13 (center left); Richard L. Carlton, 15, 21 (top right); Hjell B. Sandved, 16.

Printed in Hong Kong

1 3 5 6 4 2

CONTENTS

1
INTRODUCING SPIDERS

It's night in the backyard. The busy garden spider has begun to spin its web. The orb web begins with a strong bridge line at the top. Glistening silk spokes are added to connect the center to the bridge line and outer frame. Before long, the hard working *arachnid* will fill in the spaces between the spokes with a spiral of thin thread.

When finished, the web will be a true miracle of design, efficiency, and beauty. It may have several hundred separate attachments, and the silk may measure two hundred feet in length (61 m), yet the whole construction takes the spider about one hour to build.

THE LENGTH OF THE THREADS OF THIS GARDEN SPIDER'S WEB MAY TOTAL FROM SIXTY TO TWO HUNDRED FEET. BUT ROLLED INTO A BALL THE WEB MIGHT ONLY BE THE SIZE OF A SINGLE RICE GRAIN.

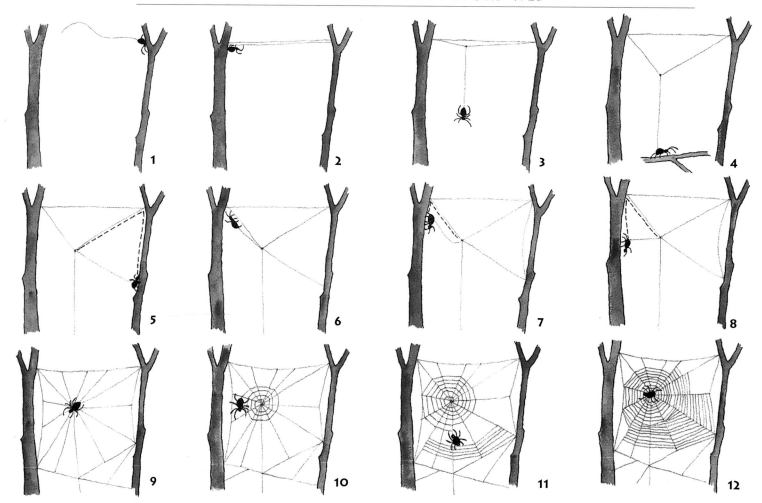

FIRST, A BRIDGE IS MADE, USUALLY WITH THE HELP OF A BREEZE (1).
THE SPIDER THEN STRENGTHENS THE BRIDGE BY WALKING BACK AND
FORTH, LAYING DOWN MORE SILK (2). THE SPIDER DROPS DOWN FROM
THE CENTER OF THE BRIDGE AND SECURES THE VERTICAL THREAD
(3, 4). FROM THE CENTER, OR HUB, OF THE WEB, THE SPIDER SPINS
SEVERAL THREADS—LIKE SPOKES IN A WHEEL—TO STRENGTHEN THE
STRUCTURE (5-9). THE SPIDER STARTS A TEMPORARY SPIRAL (10) TO
MEASURE OUT THE NEXT STAGE. IT THEN ROLLS UP THE OLD AND PUTS
DOWN NEW, MORE CLOSELY SPACED, PERMANENT SPIRALS (11 – 12).

6

After the web is complete the spider will use it to capture *prey*—insects and other small animals. Though the garden spider has eight eyes, its vision is weak. Rather than see its prey the spider feels the vibrations that it sends through the web. Once the victim is trapped, the spider quickly rushes over to bite it. Its fangs sink deep, injecting the struggling insect with a potent poison that will quickly put it out of its misery. Then the spider wraps its quarry in silk to be eaten later.

. . .

WOULD YOU LIKE TO SAVE A SPIDER WEB THAT YOU'VE FOUND? SPRAY THE WEB WITH LACQUER. THEN MOUNT IT ON A LARGE PIECE OF CONSTRUCTION PAPER.

. . .

How many insects do spiders eat? Consider that a single acre of grassland may contain up to two million spiders. If each spider traps one or two insects per day, a staggering number are being removed from the environment.

Despite all the helpful pest-control work they do, spiders are still misunderstood. Are spiders friends or enemies? In fact, while dangerous spiders such as the black widow *do* exist, the vast majority of spiders are

BABY SPIDERS
ARE BORN WITH
THE ABILITY TO
WEAVE WEBS.
THROUGHOUT
THEIR LIFETIME
THEY WILL MAKE
THEIR WEBS IN
MUCH THE SAME
WAY WITH ONLY
MINOR CHANGES.

8

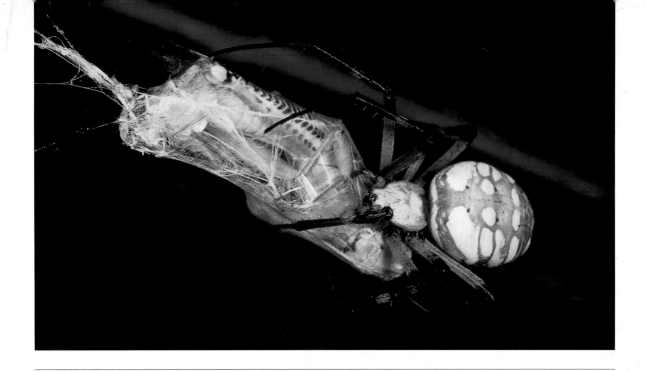

THIS BLACK AND YELLOW GARDEN SPIDER INJECTS POISON INTO A
CAPTURED GRASSHOPPER.

fairly harmless to human beings. As a threat, spiders
rank way down the list, below bees, wasps, and even
lightning strikes.

One thing about spiders that is not misunderstood
is their success as a group. In all, there are some 35,000
different *species*, or types, of spiders in the world. Spiders
have colonized nearly every land *habitat* on Earth. They
live in the hottest deserts, the highest mountain ranges,
the deepest caves, and the densest rain forests. In
general, if a habitat can support insects or other small
creatures to eat, spiders will be there.

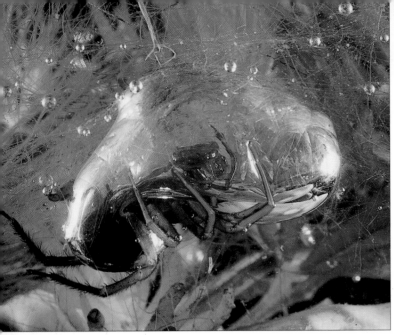

WATER SPIDERS LIVE
UNDERWATER IN
AIRTIGHT SILK NESTS

IT IS CLEAR HOW THE MEXICAN RED
KNEE TARANTULA GOT ITS NAME.
THESE COLORFUL SPIDERS HAVE
BECOME POPULAR EXOTIC PETS.

While almost every habitat is suitable for some kind of spider, every spider can *not* live in every kind of habitat. Put another way, spiders are specialized for where they live. Among the thousands of different spider species, almost every color, shape, pattern, and lifestyle imaginable exists. Spiders live in trees, on the ground, underground, and on water. There are jumping spiders, burrowing spiders, wandering spiders, and hunting spiders. Some spiders stalk their prey like hungry tigers. Other spiders live a shy existence, staying hidden for most of their lives.

THE MALE PALM SPIDER (RIGHT) MUST TREAD CAREFULLY WHEN
COURTING THE FEMALE.

Spiders vary dramatically in size. One of the world's largest spiders is the giant bird-eating spider of South America. Its leg-span would reach most of the way across the pages of this book. In contrast, the world's smallest spiders could fit on the dot of the letter i. Size also differs with respect to sex. The female wood spider, for example, can weigh up to one thousand times as much as the male of the same species!

Despite their external differences, most spiders share a number of key characteristics. They are all *predators*. They all produce silk from glands located in their abdomens and expel the silk through tiny openings in the *spinnerets*. All spiders (except one family) use their fangs to inject poison into their prey. This poison can vary in strength. In most cases, it is not strong enough to harm a human being.

Dangerous Spiders of North America

Only about 500 out of the 35,000 different spider species can be dangerous to people. However, spider bites are usually not deadly and a healthy person should recover from any symptoms after a few days. The most common dangerous spiders in the continental United States include:

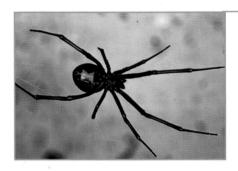

Southern black widow. Look for the red hourglass marking on the underside of the large, round abdomen. Black widows are very shy and never attack on their own. Most bites occur when people accidentally touch spiders that are in shoes, or clothing. The male is smaller than the female and light in color.

Northern black widow has two red markings on its abdomen. It is found throughout the United States, except in the Southwest.

Brown widow is found in tropical regions and in southern Texas and Florida.

Brown recluse spider or **violin spider.** Look for the violin-shaped mark on its "head." These spiders produce very painful bites but they are not life-threatening.

2
WHAT IS A SPIDER?

What makes a spider a spider? Many people mistakenly think that spiders are insects. But even though both spiders and insects are *arthropods*—animals with a hard outer skeleton and jointed walking legs—there is one clear difference between the two: insects have six legs, while spiders have eight.

How can you tell a spider from other small animals? First, as mentioned above, count the animal's legs. If it doesn't have eight legs, it is not spider. Second, take a look at the body parts. Spiders have only two: a fused head–thorax section and a lower abdomen. Next, notice the eyes. Spiders have a lot of them—from four to as many as eight, usually arranged in rows of two. In spite of this, most spiders have rather poor

THE EIGHT LEGS OF THIS GOLDEN SILK SPIDER ARE VERY SENSITIVE TO ANY VIBRATIONS PASSING THROUGH ITS WEB.

vision. Only hunting spiders have sharp enough eye-sight to use their vision to capture prey.

The fourth way to identify a spider is to take a look at how the animal eats. All spiders are predators that catch and kill prey. All spiders have fangs. All spiders (except one family) use poison to subdue their prey.

This poison can be powerful. Some spider poisons are fifteen times as strong as rattlesnake venom. However, the amount of poison that spiders inject is small. Usually, it is enough to kill an insect, but not enough to harm a human being.

The final characteristic that makes spiders unique is their ability to spin silk. It is produced by the silk glands and comes out of special structures at the end of their abdomens called spinnerets. Silk can be thick or thin, slick or sticky, depending on what it is used for. Spiders use their silk to build homes, make traps, and line *burrows*. They also use silk to wrap eggs, to serve as trip-wires or alarms, and as draglines for walking and "bungee-jumping" from place to place.

Spiders belong to a class of animals called arachnids, which also includes scorpions, ticks, and mites. There are two major orders of spiders: the

- *Spider silk is five times as strong as steel and can stretch about 30 percent longer than its original length without breaking.*
- *Many spiders build a new web every night. They recycle the silk by eating it.*

"primitive spiders," or *mygalomorphs,* and the "true spiders," or *araneomorphs.* There are about seventy spider families—eight primitive and some sixty true.

Primitive spiders are mainly large hairy spiders that look frightening but spend most of their lives hiding in underground burrows. These spiders are commonly referred to as tarantulas. This is a mistake—true tarantulas are actually a type of araneomorph.

True spiders include the spiders you are most likely to see in your own life, such as the common garden spider and daddy long-legs.

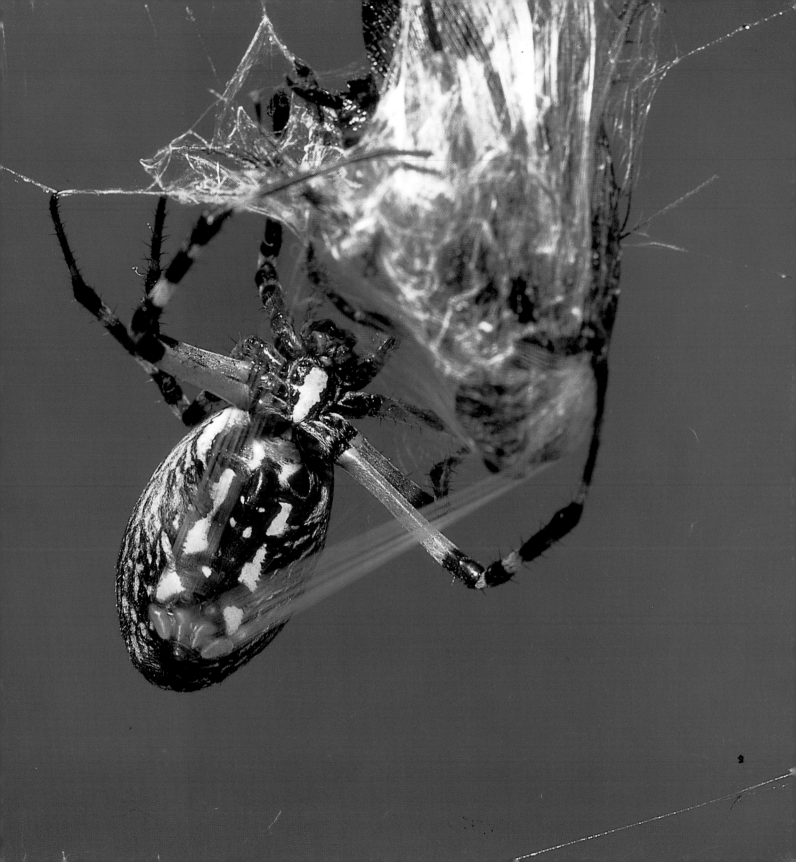

Here are examples of eight spider families that illustrate the diversity within this large group of animals.

Primitive Spider Families (*Mygalomorphs*)

Purse–web spiders hide in tubelike silk purses along the ground, which they cover with dirt. When prey walks over the purse, the spider jumps up and bites it right through the wall of the purse.

Bird–eating spiders can actually be large enough to eat small birds. They live in burrows and are mistakenly called tarantulas.

Trap–door spiders hide from their prey behind a false door.

True Spider Families (*Araneomorphs*)

Daddy long–legs spiders build sheet webs and wrap their prey before biting it.

Crab spiders have large abdomens, run sideways like crabs, and ambush their prey.

Jumping spiders have bright colors, keen eyes, and can jump twenty times their body length to catch prey.

◂ **Wolf spiders** are free-living hunters that retreat to a burrow when not active.

▸ **Orb–spinners** include the most common and well–known spiders.

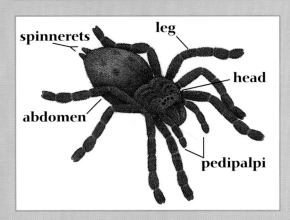

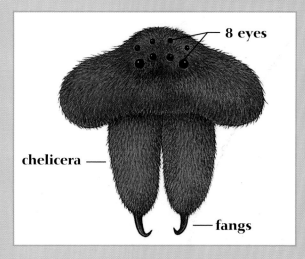

This is the body and face of a tarantula. Notice the following things that make a spider a spider: eight legs, spinnerets for spinning silk, two main sections–the abdomen and the head/thorax section. The pedipalpi look like small legs, but they are attached to each side of the spider's mouth, forming the sides of the mouth. In adult male spiders, the last of the six segments of each pedipalp bears a reproductive organ.

The chelicera, shown here, are a pair of body parts that the spider uses to seize and kill its prey. They are located above the mouth and just below the spider's eyes. The chelicera hold the poison glands that are connected to the spider's fangs.

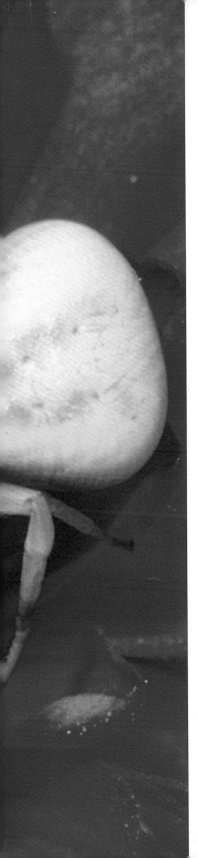

3
THE SPIDER'S WORK

The task of finding and catching prey is the daily job of every spider. Some spiders are hunters. Other spiders stay home and trap prey in their webs. Among the hunters are ambushers, chasers, jumping spiders, and pouncing spiders. Among the web–weavers are spiders that weave classic orb–shaped webs, sheet and hammock webs, funnel webs, purse webs, cobwebs, and dragline webs. Some spiders, like the spitting spiders and net-throwing spiders, fit both categories. They are web-spinners

CRAB SPIDERS ARE AMONG THE SLOWEST MOVING HUNTERS, RELYING ON STEALTH AND THE STRENGTH OF THEIR VENOM TO SUBDUE PREY. THIS CRAB SPIDER HAS CAPTURED A CRICKET.

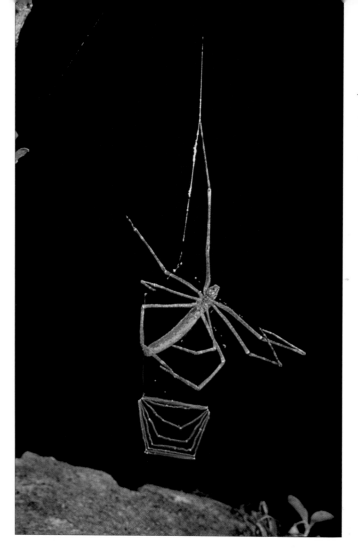

that use their webs to hunt.

Hunting spiders are typically stronger and faster than web-spinners. The hunters tend to have thick legs, keen eyesight, and powerful jaws for grabbing their prey. The web-spinners do not need strength or keen eyesight to overcome victims. They use their delicate legs to sense vibrations and navigate their webs.

Both kinds of spiders use poison to kill their victims. But different spiders use their poison in different ways. Web-spinners often wait to make sure that the victim is fully trapped before they move in for the kill. Hunting spiders need to overpower their prey.

Some use speed to gain an advantage. Others rely on the strength of their powerful jaws to subdue victims. Still others make use of the element of surprise to catch and defeat their prey. Then, like the web–spinners, they inject poison through their fangs to make the kill.

After the kill is made, both spider types inject their prey with powerful digestive *enzymes*. These enzymes eat away at the organs of the prey, reducing its insides to a thin liquid, which the spider then sucks up into its body.

THIS TRAP-DOOR SPIDER LIES IN WAIT, READY TO POUNCE ON AN UNSUSPECTING BEETLE.

Hunting Spiders

There are four main types of hunting spider: ambushers, chasers, pouncers, and jumpers. Ambushers do not chase their prey. Instead, they wait patiently for a victim to arrive. Then they attack. A crab spider may sit in a flower with its jaws open. This spider has poor eyesight but powerful venom. When a victim gets in range, it bites down hard, first stunning, then killing its prey.

Wolf spiders are chasers with strong legs and keen eyesight. When an insect comes near, these long–sighted hunters have the speed and strength to run it down. Small, active wolf spiders are commonly seen in gardens or backyards. These hunters are often very important in controlling leafhopper pests in crop fields.

Pouncing spiders build traps for their prey. The trap–door spider builds a false door that covers its burrow. When prey come across the door, the trapdoor spider quickly rushes out to make the kill. The water spider is also a pouncer. It builds an amazing under–water dome that it fills with air, bubble by bubble. When an arthropod swims by, the spider grabs it, bites it, and pulls it into its lair.

THE WATER SPIDER PASSES THE TIME INSIDE AN AIR "BELL", WAITING FOR PREY.

Jumping spiders are often brightly colored and love to bask in the sun. They have the largest eyes of any spiders. The center pair of eyes on the front of the head looks like a pair of car headlights. It is this larger pair of eyes with which the spider focuses on its prey once its movements have been picked up by the other, smaller, eyes. When hunting, a jumping spider is able to spot its victim from a distance and jump many times its own body length to subdue prey.

Web-Weaving Spiders

There are a remarkable variety of spider webs. Some webs are passive traps. Others can be used as weapons. The web of the spitting spider, for example, is a long string of sticky gum that the spider shoots at its prey. While the prey struggles, the spider comes over to administer its poisonous bite.

The ogre-faced spider uses a portable web strung

THIS LITTLE JUMPING SPIDER HAS CAPTURED A MEAL AS BIG AS ITSELF.

THE BOLAS SPIDER'S NAME
COMES FROM THE SPANISH
WORD **BOLA**, A WEAPON
USED ON THE PLAINS
OF SOUTH AMERICA
TO CAPTURE ANIMALS.
WEIGHTS ARE ATTACHED
TO THE ENDS OF A ROPE
THAT IS THROWN AT THE
LEGS OF AN ANIMAL TO
BRING IT DOWN.

between its legs to catch prey. It then hangs on a small branch, and waits for an insect to pass below. With the victim in sight the spider drops down and spreads its net over the hapless prey.

The bolas spider uses a silk "fishing line" to catch moths. The line features a drop of sticky gum on its end. The bolas spider throws the line at the moth. When the gummy end of the line strikes the moth, it sticks, and the spider reels in the prey. Scaffold-building spiders dangle sticky "fishing lines" from a flat

29

platform-type web. When an insect hits one of the sticky ends, the spider hauls it up.

More familiar webs include the classic orb-shaped web of the garden spider. The orb-weaver waits patiently for an insect to get stuck in its silk. Once it gets entangled, the spider quickly moves in to bite and wrap its victim, which it may not eat for quite a while.

Money spiders build clever hammock-shaped sheet webs that trip up insects. As the victim struggles, the spider quickly moves in from below and bites it with its fangs. Weavers of triangular webs hang from a single thread below the main web. When the prey enters the triangle, the spider pulls on its thread, trapping its victim.

Cobweb weavers, such as widow spiders, spin webs that look like a tangled mass. The silk of a cobweb is extremely strong and contains tiny loops to trip up and trap insects and other prey.

Giant wood spiders in New Guinea build webs that can be up to six feet (1.8 m) across and strong enough to trap birds. Some people have been known to use the webs of giant wood spiders as fishing nets.

THE SHEET WEB OF A MONEY SPIDER

4

THE SPIDER'S LIFE

Flying through the air with the greatest of ease, *spiderlings,* or baby spiders, are some of nature's greatest acrobats. Riding warm air currents at the end of a long silk dragline, these tiny adventurers reach altitudes of thousands of feet and can end up hundreds of miles from their original homes. This "flight" is called *ballooning.*

The spiderlings' airborne trek marks the start of another phase of the spider's life cycle—a cycle which begins during the mating season. Before mating, most spiders live independent lives. Males and females weave their own webs and hunt their own food. But when mating season comes, males begin their search for a female. Once they find one, the much smaller males have an even greater task: not ending up as dinner for their hungry female partner.

(OPPOSITE) A FEMALE INDIAN ORNAMENTAL TARANTULA STANDS CLOSE BY HER JUST-HATCHED SPIDERLINGS.

Being mistaken for prey is a very real danger for most male spiders. To avoid being eaten, males use a number of different strategies. Male jumping spiders act like cheerleaders, flashing their brightly colored *pedipalpi* to show the female that they are friendly.

COURTSHIP OF A GARDEN SPIDER: THE FEMALE (LEFT) BECOMES LESS AGGRESSIVE AS THE MALE WAVES HIS FRONT LEGS.

The wolf spider makes sounds to inform the female of its approach. Night–hunting spiders often use touch as a signal to females, tapping out a pattern that shows they are not prey. Many web–weaving males find them–selves in particular danger when they enter the female's web. If they don't produce the correct series of vibrations, their movements are mistaken for those of an insect, and the female attacks.

In some cases, such a display of good intentions is not enough. Some mygalomorph males have special leg

A MALE WOLF SPIDER (RIGHT) APPROACHES A FEMALE WITH A GIFT.

spurs that they use to lock up the female's dangerous jaws during mating. One orb-weaving spider waits to mate until the female is feeding on a recently-wrapped insect. The nursery web spider does even better than that—it brings a tasty "marriage gift" of a wrapped insect for the female to feast on. Then, while the female is distracted, the mating takes place. Crab spider males actually use silk to anchor females to the ground. Once mating takes place, the female breaks free of her silken bonds.

Even with all these careful measures, male spiders

35

are still sometimes eaten by females. This is not as great a loss as it might seem, as most males live only one year and will die soon after mating, whether they are eaten by females or not.

In any event, once eggs are laid, female spiders take care of them in a variety of ways. Most species spin egg sacs out of special silk to protect the eggs. Theradiid spiders hide their egg sacs on threads in their webs. Crab and lynx spiders attach their egg sacs under protective twigs and leaves and stand guard nearby.

Spiderlings are born as miniature adults. Some are left on their own while other spiders feed their young a kind of "milk" that is regurgitated from their own mouths. Once they are out in the world, young spiders must *disperse*, or scatter, and find new homes. Some spider species simply move on to the next burrow or rock. But many others travel as far as the wind will take them, sometimes ballooning hundreds of miles away.

Once in their new homes, spiders grow by a process called *molting*. During molting, the spider sheds its old shell to unfold a new *exoskeleton*, which it eventually grows into. Once they reach adult size most true spiders stop molting. They usually live a year or less. They are

A FEMALE CRAB
SPIDER GUARDS ITS
EGG SAC.

THIS COSTA RICAN ZEBRA TARANTULA
HAS JUST FINISHED MOLTING. THE
DISCARDED SHELL IS ON THE LEFT.

born, disperse, mate, and die all before the year is up. Primitive spiders, on the other hand, can go through many molts, and some of them live to an age of twenty years or more.

> The spiders you find in "odd" places, like bathtubs and shoes, are often males that are in search of females during mating season.

37

5
THE SPIDER'S WORLD

Some cultures recognize the importance of spiders more than others. In China, farmers build shelters to help spiders survive the cold winter. In Mexico, villagers hang tree branches covered with the webs of the mosquero spider to control swarming flies in their houses. In Belgium, beer-makers stock brewery cellars with spiders to control fruit flies.

But in the United States and many other countries, the efforts of spiders often go unappreciated. Many people think that spiders, rather than controlling pests, are the pests themselves. This results in a number of problems. Spider habitats are destroyed. Farmers spray their fields with huge quantities of insecticides that kill both insects and spiders. In 1990, sixteen spiders were

AN ORB-WEAVER RESTS ON A TROPICAL FLOWER IN PAPUA NEW GUINEA.

THIS GOLDENROD
CRAB SPIDER DOES ITS
PART TO LIMIT THE
NUMBER OF PESTS IN
ITS ENVIRONMENT.

put on the Red List of Threatened Animals by the International Union for the Conservation of Nature. Most spider experts feel that this is just a small fraction of the number of spider species that are actually in danger.

Spiders play an important role in maintaining the balance of nature—both as prey and as predator. Birds, lizards, frogs, and many other animals depend on spiders for food. Spiders, on the other hand, keep insect populations under control. Without spiders to keep things in check, the environment can suffer. For example, many insect species are designed to over-produce offspring, with only a tiny fraction of their young able to survive to adulthood. If, for example, two percent of these creatures are able to survive rather than one percent, the *ecosystem* is suddenly flooded with insects that eat crops, destroy trees, and cause other serious problems.

Some people think that the health of the spider community in an ecosystem is a good yardstick for judging the health of the entire ecosystem itself. If this is true then there is cause for real concern. Scientists have found evidence of spiders having concentrated levels of lead and other heavy metals in their bodies. More importantly, spider habitats are being destroyed or damaged at an alarming rate in today's world. Spiders themselves are being killed by over-use of chemical pesticides that are sprayed on crops. Perhaps it is time to take these threats seriously.

. . .

DO A SPIDER A FAVOR.
DO NOT BE OVERLY
NEAT IN THE YARD.
GIVE SPIDERS
PLACES TO MAKE
THEIR HOMES.

. . .

MORNING DEW HIGHLIGHTS THE BEAUTY OF A BLACK AND YELLOW GARDEN SPIDER'S ORB WEB.

arachnid: class of animals that includes spiders, scorpions, mites, and ticks; spiders are the most well-known arachnid

araneomorph: the "true" spiders that are distinguished from "primitive" spiders by their sideways jaw structure.

arthropod: animals with a hard outer skeleton and jointed legs; insects, crustaceans (crabs and lobsters) and arachnids are all arthropods

ballooning: the act of "flying" through the air while attached to a silk dragline; young spiders balloon to reach new territories (see disperse below)

burrow: an underground home that spiders and other animals (frogs, gophers) build

disperse: to avoid over-crowding in a single area, young spiders scatter or disperse to new territories shortly after they are born

ecosystem: the total environment that includes living things (plants and animals) and non-living things (rocks, water, air, etc.)

enzyme: a chemical that living things use to perform special functions such as digesting, building new tissue, and so on

exoskeleton: a skeleton that covers the outer part of the body; found on spiders and other arthropods

habitat: the place in which an organism makes its home

molting: the process of shedding the exoskeleton (or skin) to allow a spider (or other animal) to grow

mygalomorph: the primitive spiders that are distinguished from "true" spiders by their up-and-down jaw structure.

orb: the classic round "wheel and spoke" shape for a spider web

pedipalpi: a pair of appendages near the spider's head that look like small legs.

predator: an animal that eats other animals; predators eat prey

prey: the animal that is eaten by other animals; prey are eaten by predators

silk: thin material that spiders use to build webs, wrap prey, build burrows, and other tasks

species: a particular kind of organism that breeds with others of the same kind

spiderling: a young spider

spinnerets: special organs in the abdomen of a spider that produce silk

web: any structure that a spider makes out of silk

BOOKS

Biel, Timothy Levi. *Spiders*. Mankato, NM: Creative Education, Inc., 1991. A brief, basic introduction to spiders with excellent art and diagrams

Hillyard, Paul. *The Book of the Spiders*. New York: Random House, 1994. A spider–lover's account of what makes spiders special and fascinating.

Kaston, Benjamin Julian. *How to Know Your Spiders*. New York: McGraw Hill, 1978. A guide to identifying spiders.

Levi, Herbert Walter and Lorna Rose Levi. *Spiders and Their Kin*, New York: Golden Books Publishing Company, 1990. A superb guide for identifying spiders.

Preston–Mafham, Rod. *The Book of Spiders and Scorpions*. New York: Book Sales Inc., 1998. A large, handsome book that gives the reader a fairly complete view of the spider's world.

Preston–Mafham, Rod and Ken Preston–Mafham. *Spiders of the World*. New York: Facts on File, 1994. A more detailed look at spiders than the other Mafham book.

WEBSITES

The Arachnology Home Page
www.ufsia.ac.be/Arachnology/Arachnology.html
Everything you ever wanted to know about spiders and other arachnids. Includes links to other good sites.

Nick's Spiders of North America
http://members.nbci.com/nicksspiders/main.htm
Nick Loven loves spiders. His web–site is dedicated to showing pictures and photographs of North American spiders. This site will help you identify an unknown spider.

Big Spider Screen Saver
http://members.nbci.com/grandmajan/big_spiders.htm
A screen saver that you can load on your computer.

Spiders and Other Arachnids
http://www.anselm.edu/homepage/chieber/spiders.html
A few links to spider pages

Arachnida
http://www.york.biosis.org/zrdocs/zoolinfo/grp_arac.htm
Links to excellent spider web-pages. Find information about almost any spider you can think of.

ABOUT THE AUTHOR

Dan Greenberg has written numerous books for readers of all ages, on topics that range from science to math to baseball. His best-known series of humor books has ten titles, including *Comic Strip Math* and *Comic Strip Grammer*. He lives in New York with his wife and children.

INDEX

Page numbers in **boldface** are illustrations.